The Vintage Carriages Trust, based at Haworth on the Keighley and Worth Valley Railway, was formed in the early 1960's and became a Charitable Trust in 1981, registered under the Charities Act (No. 510776).

VCT owns eight historic coaches and two historic locomotives, all based on the K&WVR.

A Manchester, Sheffield and Lincolnshire Railway four wheeled tri-composite (1st, 2nd and 3rd class) of 1876. Now almost fully restored.

A Great Northern Railway six wheeled brake/3rd of 1888, fully restored externally.

A Midland Railway six wheeled composite of 1886.

A Continental brake/2nd bogie coach of 1924, built by the Southern Railway to SE&CR design. Completely restored and frequently used on special trains.

Three Metropolitan Railway bogie coaches from 1910, 1919 and 1923. Examples of the traditional wooden bodied compartment coaches used by British companies. All three have seen regular service on the K&WVR.

A 1951 built Bulleid open 3rd. After several years use, this coach is presently being extensively rebuilt.

Bellerophon, an 0-6-0 Well Tank, built in 1874 by Richard Evans and Co Ltd of Haydock Foundry for that firm's own colliery lines. One of the very earliest designs with piston valves, the locomotive is also unusual in having outside Gooch valve gear.

Extensively restored with grant assistance from the Department of Education and Science, *Bellerophon* was steamed for the first time in 23 years in May 1985.

Sir Berkeley a Manning, Wardle 0-6-0ST of 1891, used by contractors on railway construction works including the Great Central main line. Restoration is well in hand, again with Department of Education and Science grant assistance.

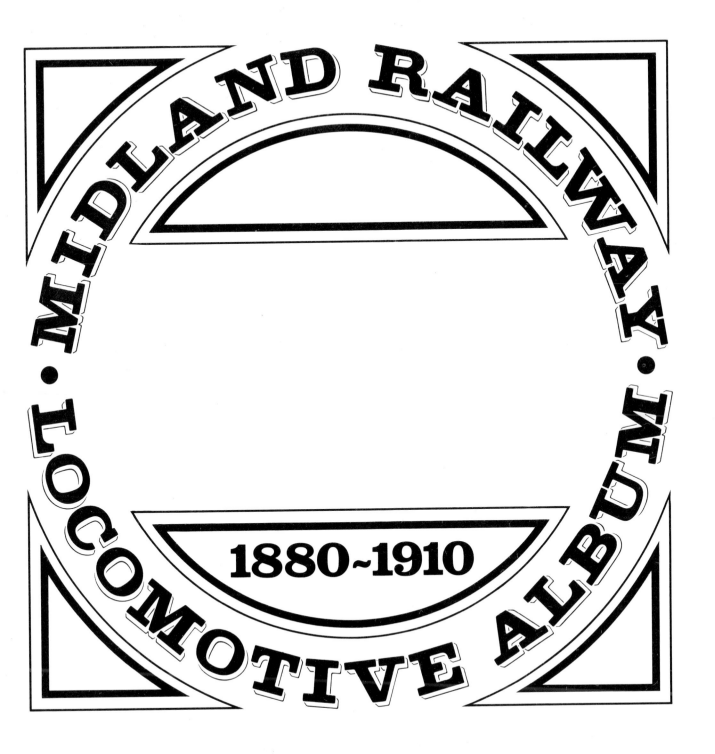

· MIDLAND RAILWAY ·
LOCOMOTIVE ALBUM
1880~1910

•

The author is a long standing member of the Keighley and Worth Valley Railway, and present editor of that Society's magazine *Push and Pull*. He is also President of the Vintage Carriages Trust, to which body the late Mr J H Wright's railway photographs were bequeathed.

John Harold Wright 1884-1978. Born into a family with agricultural interests, Harold Wright was associated with the Airedale Agricultural Society, organisers of the Bingley Show, for 75 years. The Society's Chairman from 1921 to 1932, he was also President in 1922 and 1953. A lifelong Liberal, Harold Wright was Chairman of Morton Parish Council before serving on Keighley Town Council for 21 years. He was an Alderman and Mayor for 18 months from November 1947 to May 1949, a period when a fellow railway photographer, Eric Treacy, was rector of Keighley.

One time Chairman of Bingley bench, he gave half a lifetime's service as a magistrate. Harold Wright's other great love was music and for 50 years he played the French horn with the Keighley and District Orchestral Society, serving also as President and Treasurer for a time. He was appointed a Director of the Bingley Building Society in 1923, serving as Vice President between 1939 and 1949, and from 1957 to 1963. Between these periods he was President of the Society. Following the union of the Bradford Equitable Building Society and the Bingley Building Society in 1964 he was appointed a Director of the Bradford and Bingley Society until he retired from the Board in 1970. Harold Wright was an early member of The Railway Club, joining in 1903.

The author is responsible for a previous work: a locomotive monograph "Over Here—the story of the S160's" covering the American wartime 2-8-0's which ran in Great Britain.

Compiled by Robin Higgins
Published by Vintage Carriages Trust
© Vintage Carriages Trust and Robin Higgins
ISBN 0 948530 00 6

Production by Hanson Typesetting Services Ltd, Haworth and The Crown Press Ltd, Keighley

FOREWORD

As a railway historian and lifelong railway enthusiast of catholic tastes, it always gives me much pleasure to see the appearance of a well-researched new work about the incomparable Midland Railway. One of the greatest pioneers among the railways of this country, the Midland was in several ways the most progressive when the Railways Act of 1921 brought about the loss of its separate identity in the London Midland & Scottish Railway with the dawn of 1923.

The photographs which grace this album are from the camera of the late J H Wright, who once lived near Bingley in West Yorkshire. His favourite hunting ground was the Leeds-Bradford-Skipton area, prime Midland territory and, in consequence, devotees of that railway company have benefitted greatly from his activities.

Because the photographs were taken during the years 1890-1900, an interesting period which linked the *régimes* of S W Johnson and R M Deeley, the second and third Locomotive Superintendents of the Midland, an excellent picture can be given of the gradual change in locomotive design and *décor*. The tall, majestic boiler mountings of Johnson inevitably diminished in height as boilers got bigger. Under Deeley, the livery was simplified somewhat and large, distinctive gilt numerals appeared on tender and tank sides to facilitate the operation of the first-ever British centralised train control system which the Midland introduced in 1907. But the magnificent crimson lake livery, lined-out black and edged yellow, embellished with the Company's beautiful coat of arms, remained for passenger and freight locomotives.

Over the years, Mr Wright's photographs have suffered more than a fair share of caption errors, some of which have been repeated just recently. Robin Higgins has undertaken a great deal of patient research to ensure that all the captions in this album are correct and, in other directions, has striven for a high degree of accuracy.

GEORGE DOW
Audlem, Cheshire
1985

AUTHOR'S NOTES

As a student of Midland locomotives, I have noted many conflicting statements in various publications. Where doubt has existed I have taken expert advice and am particularly grateful to Mr George Dow for reading the text and offering constructive suggestions, and to Mr Brian Radford for correcting several dimensions of the Johnson small boilered 4-4-0's. These locomotives seem to be particularly prone to confusion and have been tabulated in the hope of clarifying the many dimensional variations published over the years.

The handful of earlier photographs clearly cannot have been taken by Mr Wright but as they were in his possession from the early 1900's the belief is that they were the work of an unknown mentor, and to the author's knowledge have not been previously published.

John Harold Wright
1884—1978

To the Mayor of Keighley

from

the Rector of Keighley!

REBUILT KIRTLEY 2-4-0's

Although several of Kirtley's earlier 2-4-0's had been rebuilt by Johnson, some lasting until the 1890's, the 156 class were the earliest to survive into the 20th century and 22 received Deeley numbers in 1907. Authorities vary in the number of locomotives regarded as being 156 class. Some state that No. 156 was the first, ignoring four others built earlier the same year (1866) which had tie bars between the horns rather than the solid frames of the remainder. Two further engines were 'rebuilds' of earlier classes with new frames. No. 156 became No. 1 in 1907 and was preserved at Derby on withdrawal in 1930. Two years later, under the Stanier regime, it was cut up. Fortunately No. 2 (ex 158) having survived the second war was retained in a more enlightened era.

The driving wheels were 6'2" diameter. Originally the cylinders were 16½"x22", but from 1880 onwards rebuilding included new 18"x24" cylinders. All of the class were later put on the duplicate list and given an A suffix. Several, however, were reinstated onto the capital list and received new numbers. Some went onto the duplicate list for a second time, a few even for a third time before being given Deeley numbers. Readers are referred to British Locomotive Catalogue Vol. 3A—Moorland Publishing Co., Station Street, Ashbourne, for full details.

No. 117 at Manningham, possibly in 1886 when the locomotive was rebuilt. The absence of MR on the tender, the built-up chimney and gravity sanding all point to a date around this period. When steam sanding was introduced after 1885, the sandbox was moved from above to below the footplate. The guard irons and brake hangers are un-lined: the tender has wood faced buffer heads. The coupling rods have split brasses and cotter adjusters; these would later be replaced by one-piece bushes. No. 117 was put onto the duplicate list in 1897 and broken up in 1906.

No. 77A on the turntable at Bradford, 18 March 1905. Originally No. 111 of November 1867, it was put on the duplicate list in 1880. Restored to the capital list as No. 80 in 1888 it was duplicated again three years later. In 1895 the locomotive was again given a new number on the capital list, No. 77, and put back on the duplicate list in 1896. Deeley's renumbering finally made it No. 11 in 1907. Withdrawal came in 1928. This period saw the most elaborate lining, with the guard irons and brake hangers on both the engine and tender being lined. Compared with the previous photograph, the engine has a one-piece chimney, steam sanding, new coupling rods and a Johnson tender.

No. 154A taking water at Leeds in October 1905. Because Deeley renumbered locomotives in their order of building, No. 154A became No. 21 in 1907 and survived until 1933. The tender carries the simplified lining on the flat beading but the locomotive's guard irons and brake hangers are lined .

No. 800A, the first Neilson locomotive, at Manningham in 1905. It was put onto the duplicate list at the end of 1900, the others following over the next three years, and withdrawn in 1926.

Known as the 800 class, although the Neilson built engine carrying that number appeared three months after the first Derby engine of the class. In Kirtley's day the 800 class was renowned as the best design of express passenger locomotive. Nos. 800-829 were built in Glasgow by Neilson in 1870 (re-numbered 35-62 in 1907 in the same order, except for 801 and 807 which were broken up in 1905). Eighteen others were built at Derby, 165-169, 60-66, 3, 138, 139, 93, 22 and 23 (re-numbered 23-34 and 63-67 except for No. 3, which was also broken up in 1905). The Derby engines had lever and quadrant reversers, whereas the Glasgow ones had screw reversers. On the first ten, the screw was arranged vertically; the more usual horizontal position being adopted for the remainder. This unusual layout was held to be the main cause of a serious accident involving No. 809 setting back in thick fog after having been stopped in back gear, and the vertical screws were replaced. The class was originally allocated to Kentish Town, but was rebuilt by Johnson for use on the Settle-Carlisle line. The full length double plate frames made them sturdy, long lasting locomotives, the majority surviving into the late 1920's. As rebuilt by Johnson they shared the same B class boiler as the 156 class, the larger driving wheels diameter of 6'8" being the main difference. Because of the lack of space on the rear splasher, they were the only class to retain their number on the boilerside until transferred to the tender in 1907.

No. 810, photographed at Leeds, was one of 23 Neilson locomotives to be fitted with Westinghouse brake. The photograph is pre 1889 when Westinghouse brake was dropped (and pre 1891 due to the absence of MR on the tender). In 1884 the locomotive received a rebuild and the photograph could date from that year: there is no sign of burning on the paintwork, a common affliction of locomotives which were not recently ex-works.

No. 808A outside Leeds Station c1906.

No. 805A piloting a Belpaire at Leeds Station, 23 March 1907. A classification figure 1 has been added to the cab side.

The 890 class introduced in 1871, originally had 6′8½″ driving wheels and 17″×24″ cylinders. As with the 800 class, construction was shared between Neilson and Derby, the Glasgow firm being responsible for Nos. 890-909 (68-87 in 1907). Similarly the Derby engines were numbered in a more haphazard sequence. After Matthew Kirtley died on 24 May 1873, the remainder of the class were completed under S. W. Johnson, the last 6 receiving Johnson class P boilers from new. Only two were withdrawn prior to the 1907 re-numbering, the remainder surviving into the 1920's and early 30's. Johnson rebuilt the class, begining with No. 902 in September 1885 using new frames, 18″×24″ cylinders, and standard class P boilers, bringing them almost into line with his own designs.

No. 902 was photographed in 1907 shortly before being renumbered 80. The livery is interesting: the change from 6½″ brass numbers, on cab or boiler side, to 18″ gilt transfers on tenders commenced in April 1905. Shortly afterwards the third and final armorial design was introduced, but No. 902 still carries the second design on the cab side. No. 902 had been fitted with Westinghouse air brake. Notice the MR on the tender panel behind No. 902; this style was used only between 1898 and 1905.

No. 1072, an official Sharp, Stewart photograph in Mr. Wright's collection included to show the original appearance of the 2-4-0's. Built in 1874 as a development of the 890 class, the 1070 series were completed by Johnson. They had 6'2" driving wheels like the 156 series.

No. 136, the last of the 890 class, completed by Johnson in 1875. The elegance of Mr. Johnson's design artistry has not yet had chance to emerge. The conjoined crank splashers detract from the appearance. Other changes will involve moving the sandbox and replacing the rivetted balance weight by a crescent shaped casting. The photograph was probably taken shortly before No. 136's rebuilding at the end of 1890, the worksplate is original—and certainly before tenders began to be lettered MR. No. 136 was not placed on the duplicate list; it became No. 126 in 1907.

No. 44, a Hasland (Chesterfield) engine, in immaculate late Johnson livery. The locomotive carries a rebuilt 1901 plate and displays the full elegance of the Johnson locomotive and tender. Renumbered 118 in 1907.

JOHNSON 2-4-0's

The end of the 1870's saw the opening of important new lines to the north and south of Nottingham, putting that city on an alternative main line from St. Pancras to the north, and enabling the Midland to compete more effectively with the GNR and MS & LR for the London—Nottingham and West Riding traffic. John Noble's appointment as General Manager co-incided with the opening of these new lines and the excellent service provided by him became known as the John Noble expresses. New locomotives were built by Johnson, 30 by Derby Nos. 1400-9 and 1472-91 in 1879 and 1880 respectively (207-216 and 222-241 after 1907) and 1502-31 by Neilson (242-271).

The Glasgow engines had 6'9" diameter driving wheels; nominally ½" larger than the Derby ones. With 18"x26" cylinders and P class boilers they were powerful engines. Later rebuilds included B class boilers and most received G6 Belpaire boilers in the mid 1920's. Leeds shed had a large allocation of Neilson engines, Nos. 1502-26, the remaining five being at Nottingham. The Derby built engines, with two exceptions were all at London and Nottingham.

No. 1503 at Leeds Shed c1906. The spring buckles and brake hangers although somewhat dirty are lined, as are the guard irons but not the sand boxes. This was the first class of locomotive to have fitted from new tenders with outside sprung axleboxes with the springs below platform level.

No. 1504 shunting a corridor dining carriage, Leeds Wellington Station, 8 April 1905. Of interest is the Leeds Shed code—28—painted on the bufferbeam.

No. 1505 at Leeds Shed c1906 with simplified tender lining and lack of lining on springs, brake hangers and guard iron. The 2″ brass figure 1 on the cab side, introduced in 1905, denotes the power classification.

No. 1507 at the coaling stage, Leeds Shed. The date is certainly between 1892 and 1897. No. 1507 carries a 'rebuilt 1892' worksplate. The coal stage pilot is of particular interest. Originally an 0-4-0ST of unknown make, it was one of two 1856 built shunters taken over from Staveley Coal and Iron Co. in 1866. Numbered 207 *Ringwell*, it was put on the duplicate list in 1868 as No. 1023. In 1873 it was re-numbered 2023. The original 13″x18″ cylinders were replaced by 14″ ones in 1879 when the engine was rebuilt into an 0-4-2ST, the driving wheels remaining at 3′10″ diameter. Its last number 2023A was allocated in 1891 and the locomotive was broken up in 1897. Notice that this humble engine is vacuum fitted.

Until 1897 the passenger communication cord was strung externally along the right hand side of the train and attached to a small whistle adjacent to the main one on the firebox top. No. 1507's cord can be seen hanging on either side of the bracket midway along the tender top. The Midland introduced electric communication in 1897.

Top: Nos. 1400 and 1406 leaving Bingley with th 2pm Leeds—Carnforth train on 27 August 1907 The train consists of 11 vehicles, five 6 wheelers an six bogie carriages. The fourth carriage is a Furnes Railway vehicle. Both engines have their pre 190 numbers in large gilt figures on the tenders an whilst 1406 retains the older coat of arms, No. 140C has the new one.

Bottom Left: 2-4-0 No. 89 on the 'Little North Western' with the 2pm Carnforth express, consisting of ten or eleven vehicles. Again, the fourth one is a Furness Railway carriage.

A 2-4-0 (possibly No. 71) in the locomotive sidings just outside Leeds Wellington Station with the smokebox door open for cleaning out. In the background is an LNWR train.

Bottom Right: No. 1079 on the 12 noon Huntingdon to Kettering train near Huntingdon.

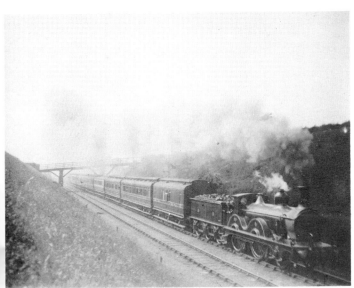

JOHNSON 4-4-0's

Class	Original numbers	1907 numbers	Date built	Driving wheel dia.	Coupled wheelbase	Cylinders	Original boiler	Builder	Notes
F	1312–1321	300–309	1876//	6'6½"	8'6"	*17½"×26"	B	Kitson	*later 18"
G	1327–1346	310–327[1]	1877	7'0½"	8'6"	18"×26"	B	Dübs	
(3)	1562–1581	328–347	1882	6'9"	8'6"	18"×26"	B	Derby	
	1657–1666	348–357	1883	"	"	"	"	"	
	1667–1676	483–492[2]	1884	7'0½"	8'6"	19"×26"	B	Derby	Joy V.G.
	1738–1757	358–377	1885/6	7'0½"	8'6"	18"×26"	B	Derby	
	1808–1822	378–392	1888	6'6½"	8'6"	18"×26"	B	Derby	
	80–87, 11, 14	393–402	1891	"	"	"	"	"	
	150, 153–5, 204–9	493–502	1897	7'0"	8'6"	18½"×26"	D	Derby	
L	2183–2202	403–422	1892	7'0"	9'0"	18½"×26"	D	Sharp, Stewart	S.V.
	156–160	423–427	1896	7'0"	9'0"	18½"×26"	D	Derby	P.V.
R	2421–2440	503–522	1899	7'0"	9'0"	19"×26"	D	Sharp, Stewart	
O	2203–2217	428–442	1893	6'6"	9'0"	18½"×26"	D	Sharp, Stewart	
	184–199, 161–4	443–462	1894	"	"	"	"	Derby	
	230–239	463–472	1895	"	"	"	"	"	
	60–6, 93, 138/9	523–532	1898	7'0"	9'6"	19½"×26"	E	Derby	
	67–9, 151/2	533–537	1899	"	"	"	"	"	
	165–169	538–542	1899	"	"	"	"	"	
T	805–9, 2636–40	543–552	1901	7'0"	9'6¹/₃₂"	19"×26"	E*	Derby	*different heating surface
	2591–2600	553–562	1901	"	"	"	E*	Neilson	
(4)	2581–2590	473–482	1900	6'6"	9'0"	18½"×26"	B	Beyer, Peacock	

(1) 1332 and 1336 were withdrawn in 1904, and 1346 was re-numbered 1336, subsequently taking that locomotive's Deeley number (318) in 1907.

(2) 1667–76 renewed with 9'0" wheelbase frames and D class boilers in 1896–1901.

(3) Derby built engines were not given class letters, but were known by order numbers.

(4) Like M & G N class C of 1898.

In 1876, the same year that his own 2-4-0's first appeared, Johnson also introduced the 4-4-0 to the Midland Railway. Ten engines of the 1312 class were not intended to be more powerful than the 2-4-0's, but rather to give experience of the riding qualities of bogie locomotives. The early 4-4-0's shared the boiler and cylinder size of the 2-4-0's, but from 1882 successively larger classes of 4-4-0 were built through to the turn of the century.

The end of the Victorian era co-incided with the last of the classically elegant designs and although Johnson introduced Belpaire 4-4-0's both simple and compound before his retirement in 1903, it was left to his successor Deeley to develop a new and handsome style. The Johnson engines were rebuilt out of all recognition by both Deeley and later Fowler with larger boilers, but many of the earlier rebuilds failed to achieve the proportioned appearance of the new larger engines.

Around 1905-09, when most of the photographs were taken, almost all types of 4-4-0 could be seen around Leeds and Bradford. Mr Wright's photographs include locomotives with each combination of driving wheel diameter and coupled wheelbase. A comprehensive list is given so that the reader can follow the twenty five years' development. The photographs are arranged in order of building even where reboilered locomotives are involved.

Thirty years old when photographed at Leeds in 1907, No. 1338 was one of a batch of twenty locomotives built by Dübs shortly after the original 4-4-0's (by Kitsons of Leeds). When built, the brass numbers were affixed in a curve, but were soon altered. Locomotives had their own headlamps, painted crimson and from 1902 carrying the locomotive number and district (prior to that date the driver's name and shed), but 1338 interestingly carries lamps lettered spare No. 3 and spare No. 4.

Above: A five year gap followed before the next batch of 4-4-0's were built. The 1562 class were identical to the 1327 class except for the 3″ smaller driving wheel diameter. No. 1577 is seen at Bradford Station c1906.

Right: Metamorphosis. The upper photograph, undated but believed to have been taken shortly after the picture of No. 2117 on 24 June 1905, shows the locomotive in its Johnson condition. In 1906, a H class boiler was fitted, transforming the appearance of the locomotive. Photographed at Leeds on 23 March 1907, No. 1579 carries the more dignified Deeley chimney and larger cab which is more in keeping with the general proportions. The new coat of arms has been applied and later in the year re-numbering to No. 345 will take place.

In 1884 Johnson had been pursuaded to use Joy valve gear on a batch of 7' 4-4-0's (1667-1676). With 19″ diameter cylinders they were a failure and despite re-building were 're-newed' eventually with new frames and larger boilers. Johnson's next class, the 1738's retained the established 18″ cylinders of his previous 7'0″ engines in the 1327 series but had the extra benefit of 160lb boiler pressure and were highly successful.

The last engine, No. 1757 gained the then unique distinction on the Midland Railway of being named. The Royal Jubilee Exhibition of 1877 was held at Saltaire and opened by Princess Beatrice, No. 1757 being named *Beatrice* in her honour. Several of the class were allocated to Leeds and Nottingham including No. 1751 which is seen shortly before being re-built with a H class boiler in 1906.

Locomotives were built in small batches for specific routes and traffic, and the driving wheel size was varied to suit. Thus for the hilly routes from Hellifield to Manchester and Liverpool, 6'6" was deemed to be suitable. Midland engines were shedded at Newton Heath (Manchester) and Sandhills (Liverpool) for working Scotch expresses over L&Y metals to Hellifield. Of the 1808 class, numbers 1808-13 went to Newton Heath, 1814-18 to Sandhills and 1819-22 to Hellifield together with the 1891 built batch.

No. 1810 on the turntable at Hellifield. The communication cord bracket can be seen on the tender, with the cord dangling down the outside of the tender. Notice the hook on the front coupling.

Top left: No. 1811 also at Hellifield around the same period. Built in 1888.

Bottom left: I couldn't resist including this photograph of L&Y 4-4-0 No. 985, at Hellifield, for comparison. Built by Beyer, Peacock in September 1888 and scrapped in 1930 as LMS 10109. An exact contemporary of Nos. 1810 and 1811 and probably photographed at the same time. The driving wheels at 6′ 0″ diameter are, 6″ smaller than the Midland ones. The cylinders are the same size at 18″ x 26″ and the L&Y engine has a firebox of 18¾ sq. ft. grate area.

Below: Rebuilt in 1904 with a H class boiler, No. 1812 was photographed at Leeds on 22 April 1905. The high pitched boiler, 'flower pot' chimney and spartan cab perched above small wheels present an un-harmonious appearance, far removed from the original Johnson symmetry. A further rebuilding took place in 1911 when, as No. 382, a G7 Belpaire boiler was fitted.

Top Right: No. 81, one of the 1891 built batch, at Hellifield with an up express on 13 June 1905 when newly rebuilt with an H class boiler.

Bottom Right: No. 11 taking water at Leeds shortly after rebuilding.

Below: No. 1809 leaving Skipton with an up express on 24 June 1906. A Hellifield engine, the quantity of coal on the tender suggests that is where an engine change took place. This locomotive had been rebuilt with an H class boiler two years previously, and in 1911 received a Belpaire boiler.

Following the introduction, in 1892, of an enlarged class of 7′ 0″ 4-4-0's which will be dealt with next , Johnson applied the same development to the 2203 class of 6′ 6″ engine built in 1893-5. The coupled wheel base was extended from 8′ 6″ to 9′ 0″ enabling a D class boiler to be used together with a modest increase in cylinder diameter to 18½″.

The engine hiding behind No. 81 on the previous page is No. 238, also newly rebuilt. Mr Wright's notes give no clue as to the identity of the train, but with modern lavatory stock it must be an important mainline connection.

No. 198, built in 1894, in fully decorated livery and including the communication whistle. This was a Durranhill (Carlisle) engine. Rebuilding took place in 1906.

No. 232 at Leeds Shed in May 1907. Rebuilt in 1904 the locomotive interestingly carries the new armorial device with the original number in transfers on the tender. Other post−1905 features are the '2' class figure on the cab side and front numberplate carried on a dished smokebox door held in position by dogs.

Right: No. 199 at Skipton on 24 June 1905. Immediately behind the tender is the turntable, which at that period was quite remote from the engine shed. In the background is the old station which was not demolished until 1967. The locomotive, newly rebuilt with H class boiler, carries the fully decorated livery: guard irons, wheel centres, bogie frame, sand boxes, brake hangers are all lined, as are the dome base and the frame section above the running plate. The tender, however, carries the new panelled style.

Numbers 233 and 235, two Leeds engines at the coaling stage. The photographs are undated but, from the state of the foliage, were not taken at the same time. No. 233 was built in 1895 and given an H class boiler in 1906. Only one whistle is carried and the lamp irons are post 1903. No. 235 was re-built in 1904 and, although a little grimy round the wheels, it is possible to see that extensive living is still carried, for example on the edge of the main frame between the bogie wheels. Both locomotives carry Leeds head-lamps with the engine number displayed thereon.

Left: No. 163 taking water at Leeds c1907. With the application of the number on the tender side the livery has been only partially simplified. The guard irons and bogie frame still carry lining although other features do not. The smokebox appears to be of the flat pattern. The gentleman with white whiskers and bowler hat standing between No. 163 and No. 1841 appears on several of Mr Wright's photographs and may have been the shed foreman.

In 1892 the wheelbase of the 7' 0" 4-4-0's was extended by 6" to 9' 0", enabling the larger D class boiler to be fitted. Sharp, Stewart & Co. built 20 locomotives, the 2183 class. Johnson had kept to 18" diameter cylinders for all engines including the 2183 class after the Joy valve gear 1667 class with 19" cylinders proved to be costly failures. However, experience with the 2183's pursuaded Johnson that larger cylinders could be fitted and a Derby batch built four years later in 1896 had a modest increase to 18½" diameter. These engines were the first 4-4-0's to have piston valves. The 1667 engines, rebuilt in the meantime but still not satisfactory, were 'renewed' with new 9' 0" wheelbase frames and D class boilers between 1896 and 1901 bringing them into line with the 156 class. Further batches followed in 1897—10 engines, and 1898—20 engines. No. 2434 is a Sharp, Stewart engine of 1892 on the turntable at Leeds c1907. In the background is a LNWR 2-4-0. A Leeds engine, it was re-built in 1908.

No. 1670 at York on 13 July 1907. Notice the engine number and shed allocation painted on the buffer beam: a peculiarity of Nottigham−1670's shed, and Sheffield. Renewed in 1901, rebuilding took place in 1908.

In the final development of the classic Johnson 4-4-0, the 60 class introduced in 1898, the wheelbase was extended to 9' 6" to accomodate the E class boiler used on the 115 class 4-2-2's of 1896. This was pressed to 170 psi and had a grate area of 21. 3 sq. ft. The class of thirty locomotive was constructed in batches up to 1901. By this time the growth in traffic, and particularly the introduction of heavy dining carriages, necessitate extensive double heading of express trains. The Midland Board were forced to accede to the building of large locomotives and the introductio of the Belpaire 4-4-0's in 1900 rendered the later engines obsolescent from the start. Re-building with H class boilers began within five years.

No. 2639, built in 1901, at Leeds Shed c1906 shortly before re-building. Although in the fully lined livery, the paintwork is less tha pristine and shows signs of flaking off the firebox side. A Johnson class 1F 0-6-0T is coal stage pilot in the background.

No. 169 at Leeds Wellington in March 1907, with the original number now applied in gilt transfers to the tender, and flat smokebox door with cast numberplate.

Top Left: No. 806 at Holbeck Shed, Leeds; built in 1901 and photographed shortly before re-building in 1906.

Bottom Left: No. 806 again at Holbeck c1907, soon after having been re-built. The larger cab is more appropriate and the chimney more elegant than the 6′ 6″ re-builds.

Below: Sister engine No. 805 is photographed just inside Holbeck roundhouse, around the same time. Notice the signal on the wall.

No. 2595 at Leeds Wellington at the head of the 4 pm St. Pancras express on 23 March 1907. The locomotive had only just been re-built and was ex-works.

JOHNSON SINGLES

Chronologically, the Johnson Singles come after both the 2-4-0's and 4-4-0's. Kirtley had abandoned single wheelers in favour of 2-4-0's in 1866 due to slipping problems. At that time, sanding was by gravity and the 2-2-2's were finding increasing loads a problem. The introduction of steam sanding—a Derby invention—in 1885, brought about a revival of the single wheeler, with the building of No. 25 in 1887, the first of 95 Johnson 4-2-2's in five classes. At that time, locomotive tyres were softer and less consistent in composition than in later years and uneven wear on four coupled locomotives could cause heating problems. 'Spinners', as they were called, were never seen North of Leeds; their characteristics being suited to the older main lines with lesser gradients. They *were* used on the Bristol main line; the Lickey incline, however, demanded that all expresses to the end of steam required banking assistance over that short distance.

By 1900, ever increasing train loads brought an end to the development of the Johnson Spinners, culminating in the 'Princess of Wales' class weighing 50 tons.

THE JOHNSON SINGLES

Original number series	1907 numbers	Date built	Driving wheels	Cylinders	Boiler class	Notes
25–32	600–607	1887/8	7'4"	18"×26"	D	
1854–7, 37	610–614	1889				
1858–62	615–619	1889/90				
1853, 34	608, 609	1889	7'6"	18½"×26"	D	
1863–72	620–629	1889–91				
8, 122, 20*, 145, 24, 33, 35, 36, 38	630–638	1891–3				*Renumbered 132 in 1900
39, 4, 16, 17, 94, 97, 98, 99, 100, 129	639–648					
133, 149, 170–8	649–659					
179–183	660–664	1893	7'6"	19"×26"	D	piston valves
75–7, 79, 88	665–669	1896				
115–121	670–676	1896/9	7'9"	19½"×26"	E	118 preserved piston valves
123–128	677–682	1899				
130/1	683, 684					
2601–5, 2606/7/8*	685–692	1900	7'9½"	19½"×26"	F	*Renumbered 19, 20, 21 in 1900 piston valves
22–3	693, 694					

Left: In the mid to late 1890's under Robert Weatherburn, the London District Locomotive Superintendent, six or seven Kentish Town Singles were favoured with a non-standard livery which included additional lining. No. 1862, built in 1890 was one such locomotive. The upper photograph was taken at Kentish Town Shed prior to the engine being re-built in 1902. Lining extends to guard irons, axle ends and wheel centres, bogie frames and bolster, sand box side and end, brake hangers; spring hangers, buckles and top and bottom leaves; main frames, motion bracket; dome and safety valve base; and of especial note the panel on the splasher top and V's on the wheel spokes. The underside of the boiler is painted cream to reflect light onto the motion, which appears to be bright steel. The pristine condition in which the engine was kept may account for the lack of a visit to the paint shop for the 'MR' to be applied to the tender.

The lower photograph is dated c1906 after removal of the communication whistle and smokebox lamp bracket. The locomotive, standing at the head of a St. Pancras corridor express in Leeds Station, carries a re-built 1902 workplate. Although most of the Weatherburn lining is still present, including the cream underside of the boiler, the spokes, axle ends and splasher top are no longer lined.

Below: Contrasting with the previous photographs, No. 1867 is distinctly grubby and entirely devoid of below footplate lining—except on the tender frames. Photographed at Leeds Shed in May 1907 with the final coat of arms, old number in transfers and '1' cabside classification. This was the final Single to have outside plate springs for the driving wheel; subsequent engines having twin helical springs.

The outstations at Manchester and Bristol also deviated from standard lining. No. 39 was photographed at Bristol with unfinished paint-work on the front sandbox and brakehangers. Points of difference include the V's on the bogie frame and fancy lining on the rear spring hangers. The dome base has double lining. The locomotive carries a re-built 1899 plate.

No. 37, also a Bristol engine and carrying a re-built 1902 works-plate. Another point of difference from the London style is the double lining on the sandboxes. The front as well as the top of the motion bracket is lined. The communication whistle is still present although the cord bracket is missing from the tender: the smokebox lamp bracket has also been removed. How magnificent these engines must have looked in comparison with others seen at Bristol.

No. 689 (old 2605) being coaled at Leeds in 1907. Shed allocation plates had recently been introduced, 16 being Kentish Town. Originally the locomotive was based at Nottingham.

Train spotters of 1907 must have been confused by locomotive No. 20 paired with No. 21's tender. The 11.40 down Scotch passes Mill Hill.

THE BELPAIRE 4-4-0's

The appearance of the first Belpaire 4-4-0's in September 1900 caused howls of protest from the locomotive connoisseurs of the day. Gone were the elegant curves of the driving wheel splashers, the slender boiler and shapely safety valve casings. But in retrospect the overall appearance is neat and handsome, marred perhaps by the attenuated cab which Deeley would put to rights. Almost all the class received extended smokeboxes, and almost all of those were superheated commencing in 1913. Many later received 20½" cylinders. Twenty survived the war to be allocated BR numbers, but only eight actually received them, the last one No. 40726 (old 816) going in September 1952.

Numbers series 2606-10 (700-4), 800-4 (705-9), 2781-90 (710-9), 810-69 (720-79). Driving wheel diameter 6' 9", coupled wheel base 9' 6", grate area 25 sq. ft. Cylinders 19½" x 26", boiler pressure 175 psi (last 10, 200 psi).

No. 2606, the doyen of the class, stands well coaled up in Leeds Wellington station on 14 October 1905.

No. 2606 at Leeds on 14 October 1905. The main frames and bogie frames are lined together with the dome base. The first ten Belpaires varied in detail from subsequent batches: the GX boiler was 6″ shorter than the G8 employed later, no steps were provided behind the bogie, and the rear splasher is less tall. Notice that the driver's right arm is resting on the hand rail at the height subsequently adopted for the splasher. The splasher guard behind the sandbox, between the bogie and driving wheels can clearly be seen.

No. 821 in the repair shop at Leeds. It had been running with compound No. 2634's tender—visible beneath the boiler— whilst 2634 had 821's tender. May 1907 .

Goods locomotives ran in unlined livery but Belpaires did not. No. 2608 has probably been steam tested before final painting and lining. As it carries both the smokebox lamp bracket and communication whistle, it may have been newly built.

The slow film emulsion available made photography of moving trains difficult. Perhaps Mr Wright had made arrangements with the driver; certainly the chimney exhaust is wet and the cylinder taps are closed. The photographer has caught the engine on its first exhaust beat, after moving 5′ 6″ from rest, and the result is a sharp picture. No. 823 at the head of the 2.25 Leeds−St. Pancras on 16 September 1905.

No. 810 at Carlisle and No. 827 [at] Leeds, both displaying the earl[y] lining style on the tender. Both ha[ve] wheel centre lining and tend[er] springs, axlebox covers and fram[es] lined. No. 827 was photograph[ed] c1906, and No. 810, still carrying th[e] communication whistle, somewh[at] earlier.

No. 823 at Holbeck on 7 April 1906. A 1903 built locomotive, it exhibits detail changes compared with the first batch. The rear splasher is taller, front steps have been provided, and a retrograde alteration has been made in the visual appearance of the chimney. Covers for the wash out plugs on the firebox side have been provided.

A cab view of Belpaire No. 827 in Leeds roundhouse. Notice that only one water gauge frame is fitted, on the left, with two test cocks on the right. The Midland combined steam/vacuum brake valve, later adopted as standard by the LMS, was a familiar fitting on Fowler and Stanier locomotives built up to nationalisation.

Belpaires were very rarely seen on the Little North Western line, except on the special Saturdays and Mondays only Isle of Man dining corridor train from Heysham to St. Pancras. Believed to be No. 845.

9.45am St. Pancras—Glasgow express near Bingley on 27 August 1907. Old number 836 re-numbered 726.

No. 2781 at Hendon on the 10am down Manchester express.

No. 767 paired with 761 tender on a down Leeds and Bradford express.

THE COMPOUNDS

There is no doubt that S. W. Johnson was in the vanguard of locomotive development with the introduction of the first Midland Compound on 6 November 1901. Numbered 2631, it was described as an ugly brute until the drivers quickly found what a remarkable machine they had been given. A sister engine, No. 2632, was also working before the end of 1901 although officially regarded as 1902 built. The main difference was in the tube arrangement, the former having 1¾" plain copper tubes and the second engine 2¾" Serve internally ribbed tubes. The grate area was 26 sq. ft. and boiler pressure 195 psi.

As independent reversers were provided for hp and lp valves, each locomotive was at first in the exclusive charge of one particularly able driver. Not for the last time, extensive testing was carried out on the Settle—Carlisle line and remarkable performances resulted. Steaming was excellent, with good coal economy and the ability to run hard up hill and fast down hill. Ais Gill summit was breasted at up to 43 mph southbound with 250 ton trains and speeds as high as 96 mph achieved in Ribblesdale.

Three further Compounds appeared in 1903 shortly before Johnson retired, numbered 2633-5; they had a straight footplate with no raised sections over the cylinders. In the interests of practical day to day working, no independent control of hp and lp valves was provided.

The first Deeley Compound appeared in 1905, their curved rear splashers and canopied cab producing a harmonious appearance. Deeley's specially designed regulator valve enabled straightforward operation. Although Deeley urged the adoption of superheating at the time, such was the royalty charge that it was not until 1913 that the first Compound was so fitted. An enlargement of the grate area to 28.4 sq.ft. and increase in boiler pressure to 220 psi were two important changes from the original Johnson engine. After 1905, under the strict traffic control scheme of Guy Granet and Cecil Paget, train loads were rigorously limited and exceptional performances became rare until LMS days. The Midland bequeathed 45 Compounds to the LMS and in comparative tests with LNWR and Caledonian types, the Compounds proved to be superior. No fewer than 195 further Compounds were built by the LMS between 1924 and 1932. All 240 were inherited by BR although 13 of the Midland ones were withdrawn before being re-numbered.

No. 1008 on Leeds shed.

No. 2631, the doyen of the class, in Holbeck roundhouse c1905. Notice the two reversing levers for independent control of hp and lp cylinders. On the smokebox side is the valve for regulating admission of live steam to the two outside (lp) cylinders.

No. 2631, later No. 1000, at Leeds. Johnson's five Compounds were originally numbered 2631-5. Deeley's Compounds commenced at 1000 and had reached 1029 by December 1906. The 1907 re-numbering scheme changed 2631-5 to 1000-4 and the Deeley engines had their numbers increased by 5. Thus 1000 became 1005 and 1029 became 1034. Fortunately no further Compounds were built until November 1908 thus limiting possible confusion.

No. 2634, built in September 1903, was the fourth Compound to enter service. The three 1903 locomotives were sent to Kentish Town shed to work expresses to Leeds. No. 2634 is in charge of the 3.45 non stop from Leeds to St Pancras

No. 2634 on arrival at Leeds from St. Pancras. A point of interest is the red panel on the front splasher.

No. 2634, carrying the 1905 armorial device, and running with the tender from Belpaire 4-4-0 No. 821.

No. 2633 at Appleby c1906 on an up train. The photographer's caption claims it to be a Glasgow-Leeds express, but the two lamps which are visible—smokebox top and left buffer—point to a special working. Notice the absence of Johnson regulating valve from the smokebox.

No. 1004 (2635) at Leicester
28 December 1909.

No. 1008 on shed at Leeds on
7 April 1906.

No. 1012 at St. Pancras when newly built in 1906.

No. 1028 at Holbeck shed.

No. 1014 at Leeds when new in 1906.

No. 1032, originally 1027, shortly after re-numbering in 1907. Built in 1906 and scrapped in 1952 from Nottingham shed. Photographed at Leeds coaling stage.

No. 1014, later 1019, departing from Leeds in 1906 with a St. Pancras express.

THE 0-4-4 TANK ENGINES

S. W. Johnson had built 0-4-4T's for the Great Eastern Railway and he introduced his own design to the MR in 1875 with the 6 class. The C class boiler used had a grate area of 16 sq. ft. and at first 140 psi sufficed; being raised later to the 150 psi of the 1889 built engines. A larger driving wheel diameter was used on the thirty members of the 1252 class, introduced later the same year, 5' 6" instead of 5' 3", but all later batches reverted to the original size. In 1881 the 1532 class, totalling 65 engines over five years, were introduced. These originally had 17" x 24" cylinders and 140 psi pressure. They are sometimes lumped together with the subsequent 100 locomotives, but these, the 1823 class, were built from new with 18" cylinders and 150 psi pressure. Also the last 50 locomotives, when built, had a modified C1 boiler of the same grate area but 4" deeper firebox, and the water capacity was 1270 gallons compared with the 1,000 or 1150 gallons of the earlier engines.

The 0-4-4T's were successful locomotives, capable of a good turn of speed. 201 of the 205 built were still in traffic at the end of the Midland Railway's independent existence on 31 December 1922, and 61 were bequeathed to British Railways. No. 6, when withdrawn at the end of 1930, was intended for preservation but with the advent of the Stanier era two years later it was cut up. Although the last of the 0-4-4T's survived into 1960 no further preservation attempt was made.

No. 1266 at Bradford, one of the Neilson built 5' 6" series from 1875. As a rule these engines worked bunker first to Leeds.

No. 1636 and 1641 at Manningham. 5′ 3″ engines built in 1883 and 1884 respectively, both locomotives are immaculate and probably brand new. No. 1636 was the last new Midland locomotive to be painted green. With the photographic emulsions then available green and red were indistinguishable on photographs, but it may be that the photographs were taken with the specific hope of showing the old and new colours.

The style of lining is identical, with the dome base, sand boxes, buffer planks and wheel centres lined, but not the guard irons or brake hangers. Notice the bottle jacks carried on the side tank, and the small passenger communication whistle adjacent to the main one. Both locomotives carry the extra lamp brackets of pre-1893. A minor difference is the additional coal rail on 1636. The handful of the 1532 class to survive nationalisation included both 1636, which was allocated 58044 but scrapped in April 1948, and 1641 which became 58045 and was broken up in October 1951.

Top Left: No. 1841 taking water at Leeds Wellington. LNWR 2-4-0 *Theorum* is in the background. Built in 1892, this engine became an early casualty, being withdrawn at the end of 1928.

Bottom Left: No. 2626, a 1900 built engine in No. 2 Platform at St. Pancras.

Bottom Right: Also at St. Pancras No. 2219, a condenser fitted locomotive for working over the Metropolitan lines to Moorgate Street. The white square board with diagonal black cross hooked onto the front would be carried on one of the front lamp brackets to signify the train's destination when working over the City and Suburban lines. Full details are given in George Dow's book Midland Style. The locomotive carries the special headcode for an ECS working from St. Pancras to Cattle Dock Sidings, Kentish Town.

This Page Top: No. 1546 at the 'coal hole', Manningham c1906 in full crimson livery with even the guard irons and brake hangers lined out. These engines worked expresses of up to ten bogies (200-230 tons) between Leeds and Bradford, reaching speeds of 65 mph.

Bottom: A side view of No. 1546 coupling onto an express at Leeds for the remainder of the journey to Bradford. Chimney first working out of Leeds was the rule. Notice how the paint has been burnt off the boiler cladding around the clack valve.

When this photograph of No. 1546 was taken on 23 March 1907, the dished smokebox door with centre fixing had been replaced by the Deeley flat door secured by seven dogs, introduced in 1905. The lining has been simplified and is missing from the top and end of the buffer plank, and the bottom of the footplate angle.

Aire Valley locals near Bingley, consisting of five close coupled Clayton clerestory bogie coaches with a brake at each end. The top photograph was taken on 13 June 1905 and the bottom one on 27 August 1907.

0-6-0 TENDER LOCOMOTIVES

The vast numbers of Kirtley and Johnson 0-6-0's make it impossible to list them in this volume. Many of the earlier Kirtley engines, with their strong double frames, withstood re-building with larger cylinders and bigger boilers pressed to higher pressures. Engines from the 1850's survived into LMS days and one, Kitson built No. 401 (later 421) of 1857 after being withdrawn as LMS 2385 was restored for preservation only to be cut up in 1932. A lost opportunity occurred at the end of 1951 when the last Kirtley double framed 0-6-0 with Johnson round top firebox was withdrawn as BR 58110. Having outlived all the others by 20 years it seems reasonable to imagine that someone in a position of influence at Derby had hung on to this venerable relic, finding suitably light work for it, in the hope that those in a position of power would preserve old No 778 of 1869. Alas, it was not to be: steel was in short supply and there were BR Standards to build.

Until 1852, Kirtley's 0-6-0's had sandwich frames; thereafter plate frames being adopted. The wheelbase of the earlier engines was 8' + 8' extended in the mid 1850's by 3" and lengthened by the same amount in 1858 to produce the first of a very long line of classes with 8' + 8' 6" wheel base. A change from straight top to curved frames occurred in 1863.

Johnson's 0-6-0's, all inside framed, came in two wheel sizes, 4' 10" and 5' 2½", the smaller ones mostly remaining as class 2's, while the 5' 2½" engines tended to be re-boilered and become class 3. Many, but not all, went through the stage of having H class round top boilers fitted before a second re-building with Belpaire boilers. Some were downgraded from 3 to class 2 with G 6 boilers. The 1907 re-numbering-retained in 1923-made no distinction between power classes. It was left to BR to segregate them, when adjacent engines such as 3489 and 3490 became 58270 (class 2) and 43490 (class 3). At the end of 1922 there were 453 Johnson class 2 engines, 482 Johnson and Deeley class 3's together with 471 Kirtley engines.

No. 567, one of a batch of 15 built in 1866 by Kitson of Leeds (555-69). A members of the 480 class introduced in 1863, the second standard Kirtley goods class which was built by Sharp, Stewart; Dübs; and the Yorkshire Engine Co., as well as Kitson and the Midland Railway itself. Driving wheels 5' 2½" diameter; wheelbase 8' + 8' 6". Cylinders originally 16½" x 24", 17" from 1880. Renumbered 2506 in 1907 and condemned in 1925. Some of the batch went as early as 1902, the last going in 1931. No. 567 was re-built in 1897 and was probably photographed shortly before this date. Notice the hook on the front coupling and the wooden headed tender buffers.

No. 415, one of the earlier Kirtley straight framed locomotives, built by Robert Stephenson in 1859. Re-built by Johnson in 1893 and photographed at Manningham shortly before withdrawal in 1903. One or two of the class survived into early LMS days. This was one of the earliest engines with the 8' + 8' 6" wheelbase which became the Midland standard through to 1922 and beyond into the Stanier era.

No. 582 outside the wooden straight shed at Manningham around 1905. This was one of 18 Derby built engines from 1866. Numbered 2488 in 1907, it was condemned at the end of 1930.

No. 1224 at Dent on an up pick-up goods. The substantial sleeper fences in the background were intended to protect the line from drifting snow. Built by Neilson in 1876 the locomotive survived until August 1960, as BR 58165; almost all of the class of 30 received BR numbers.

Sharp, Stewart built No. 2121 at Manningham on 31 March 1906 displaying the closer spaced MR on the buffer beam. Withdrawn at the end of 1959 as 43398. Manningham station is in the right background.

Two views of No. 1357 taken within a few minutes of each other at Bradford Forster Square in 1905, showing how the full lining is more visible from the rear view. The first of the larger (5′ 2½″) wheeled 0-6-0's; built by Dübs in 1878. Others came from Stephenson, and Beyer, Peacock as well as Derby. Originally built with 17½″ cylinders, 18″ ones were fitted in 1893. In 1921 a Belpaire G 6 boiler was substituted and as LMS 3020 the engine was withdrawn in 1927. Other members of this group of twenty lasted as late as November 1959.

No. 1606 on shed. A Beyer Peacock 5' 2½" locomotive with that company's style of tender. Painted in the fully lined livery and photographed c1906. Notice the SHE of Sheffield on the front buffer beam. Whilst others of the class lasted into the 1960's, No. 3104, as it had become, was withdrawn at the end of 1936.

In contrast No. 1229, photographed around the same time is unlined. The livery would be the plain crimson lake or red brown adopted during the great locomotive shortage at the turn of the century. One of the 1142 class of 4' 10" locomotive introduced in 1875 and built by Kitson; Dübs; Beyer, Peacock and Neilson. Built in 1876, this Neilson engine received a G 6 boiler in 1917. Re-numbered 2997 in 1907 it survived, along with 23 others of this group of 30 engines, into BR days being withdrawn in 1960 as 58170.

No. 2304, a Neilson 5' 3" locomotive of 1896. Re-built in 1904 with a H class boiler, it moved up from class 2 to class 3. Photographed in fully lined livery in c 1905. Re-numbered 3490 in 1907 and fitted with a G 7 Belpaire boiler in 1924. Finally withdrawn at the end of 1959 as 43490. Others of the class received G 6 boilers and remained class 2; for example No. 2303 (3489 in 1907) which became BR 58270.

No. 2158 looking rather grubby at Carlisle Durranhill shortly after re-building with an H class boiler in 1903. Built by Dübs in 1893, a 5' 3" locomotive which received a G 7 boiler in 1923; became No. 3435 and BR 43435; and was withdrawn in 1962. Again others of the class remained as class 2 with G 6 boiler, and became BR 58XXX series.

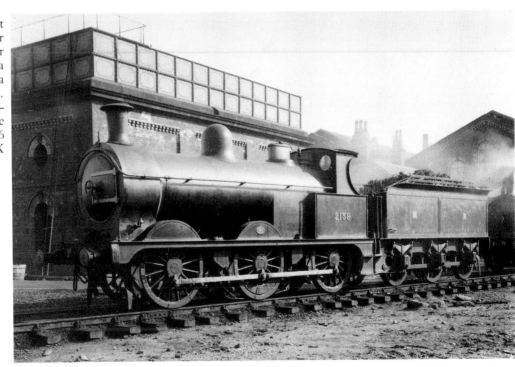

No. 2113 at Skipton shed. Believed to be newly delivered from Sharp, Stewart in 1892. Notice the disposition of the five lamp brackets and the peculiar Midland front coupling with the hook on the end of the three links. No. 2113 followed the common pattern of re-building with an H boiler but was withdrawn as No. 3390 in 1925 without receiving a Belpaire boiler. Others did receive G 6 or G 7 boilers, and survived into the 1950's and 60's respectively.

No. 2117, another Sharp, Stewart 1892 locomotive, at Skipton Station South Junction on 24 June 1905. Rebuilt the same year with an H class boiler, it carries the newly introduced class 3 figure underneath the number. A further re-building took place in 1922 when, as No. 3394, a G 7 boiler was fitted. Withdrawal came in 1962 as 43394.

No. 1787, an example of a locomotive carrying its pre 1907 number in transfers on the tender and the final coat of arms on the cab side. A Derby built 4' 10½" locomotive built in 1887 and fitted with an H class boiler in 1905. Re-numbered 3179 in 1907. Down graded to class 2 in 1925 when a G 6 boiler was fitted, it was withdrawn the same year.

No. 2116, yet another Sharp, Stewart 1892 locomotive photographed when new complete with the original maker's plate, five lamp irons and lack of conventional drawhook. An early casualty, the engine was withdrawn in January 1928 without being re-built.

No. 2180 believed to be at Leeds coaling stage when newly re-built with H class boiler in 1904. Built by Dübs in 1893 and re-built with a G 7 Belpaire boiler in 1921, the locomotive was withdrawn in mid 1960 as BR 43457. The engine is immaculately turned out in the plain unlined red livery with black splasher tops and beading, and black boiler bands.

A 5′ 3″ 0-6-0 on passenger work, photographed near Bingley with a five coach Aire Valley set strengthened with three additional carriages. Described by the photographer as an excursion, and taken on 12 June 1905.

THE AMERICAN 2-6-0's

A strike in the locomotive building industry in 1899 occurred at a time of general trade expansion and the Midland together with the Great Northern and Great Central were obliged to turn to America for the supply of locomotives. Two builders supplied 'off the peg' designs of small 2-6-0's almost identical to locomotives exported to such countries as Egypt and Finland. Both builders delivered their orders within a few weeks and the designs were pure American except for buffers and couplings. Both designs employed bar frames, 18″ × 24″ outside cylinders supplied with steam at 160 psi, and 5′ 0″ diameter driving wheels. The ten Schenectady engines had sandboxes located below a relatively low running plate with small, neat splashers. A distinctly Midland looking 6 wheeled tender completed the ensemble. The thirty Baldwin locomotives, on the other hand, had bogie tenders, running plates clear of the wheels, the forward sandbox in the shape of a dome on the boiler top and stay bars between the smokebox and buffer beam. The spacious looking cabs in fact housed the rear of the firebox for half their length. After completion the locomotives were dismantled for crating, and reassembled at Derby, the Baldwin ones out-of-doors such was the pressure on erecting shop space: fortunately it was a good summer.

Contemporary reports claim that the American engines were not popular. Coal and oil consumption and repairs were quoted as being 20% 50% and 60% respectively higher than the contemporary Derby 0-6-0. But repairs of any small group of non standard locomotives would be expected to cost more compared with thousands of standard ones. The fact that the American engines were withdrawn by 1914 does not imply that the design or workmanship were poor. By that date the fireboxes would be up for renewal and as bar frames were thicker than plate frames, the American boilers would have narrower fireboxes. Midland boilers could not be fitted in American frames so the engines were scrapped. The deeper fireboxes and hence thicker fires could account for higher coal consumption coupled with the probable lack of dampers. Higher oil consumption suggests bigger bearing surfaces; or that drivers were not removing trimmings from oil boxes when not in use. The author's experience with the later USA locomotives suggests that as machines with good availability and ease of maintenance, they were in no way inferior to British products; and indeed the American locomotive industry captured many British export markets.

Left: No. 2515 on a coal train. One of the Schenectady locomotives, photographed shortly after delivery with the earlier layout of five lamp brackets and carrying lined livery. Notice that the tender does not have a vertical central beading and hence the lining is in one large panel. All ten engines were based at Wellingborough. Traditional American doors were fitted to the cab front, allowing easy access to the running plate. No. 2515's driver's side door is open.

Previous Page Right: No. 2527 at Lancaster shed with 0-4-4T No. 2617 in the background.

This Page Top: No. 2534 at Leeds shed, a post 1905 photograph of a Baldwin engine.

Bottom: A Schenectady engine on the main line with a mineral train.

The Midland had quite a collection of odd industrial 0-4-0 and 0-6-0 tank engines seized from their previous owners for non payment of debts. No. 2069A was built by Hunslet Engine Co. of Leeds for the Erewash Valley Iron Co. of Trowell in 1880. The Midland acquired it five years later, allocating the number 1697. Put on the duplicate A list in 1890, it was further re-numbered in 1892 as 2069A. Well known as the Manningham shed shunter it is seen there with the coal stage and square roundhouse in the background. Its livery is unlined crimson lake and the date is shortly before being withdrawn in January 1903.

There were twenty of these little 0-4-0ST's. Ten were built in two equal batches in 1883 and 1889/90, with 3′ 9½″ diameter wheels at a wheelbase of 7′ 0″. Cylinders were 13″ x 22″ and weight 21 tons 14 cwt. These were followed by ten more again built in two equal batches in 1893 and 1897 with the same dimensions as the previous engines but slightly heavier at 22 ton 19 cwt. No. 2359 was the first of the 1897 batch and was one of two engines built on the capital account, the others being given a suffixed number from new and built out of the revenue account. The penultimate engine surprisingly survived until 1955 as BR 41516, the other nine having been withdrawn between 1921 and 1936.

No. 2359 carries a single line round the tank and bunker/number panel. Notice the bell mounted on the tank front alongside the chimney; a legal requirement for working on public roads.

No. 1514, previously 2360, at Leeds shed, post 1907 with simplified lamp brackets and carrying a shed plate (28) on the smokebox door.

In the early 1870's the 3′ 8″ tramways and 7′ 0¼″ lines of the Severn and Wye were gradually abandoned or converted to standard gauge. Three 0-6-0T's were built by Fletcher Jennings & Co. for the new standard gauge lines and named *Will Scarlet*, *Little John* and *Alan-a-Dale*. Passenger services were introduced on some of the lines in 1875 and after amalgamation with the Severn Bridge Railway in 1879, the company was vested jointly in the GWR and Midland in 1894. In the following year the total of 19 locomotives was shared, and the Midland found itself with *Little John*. With 4′ 0″ driving and 16″ x 24″ outside cylinders, *Little John* had been re-built at Lydney in 1894 and subsequently became No. 1123A of the Midland Railway before being broken up in 1905. It is seen here at Derby works in plain crimson lake livery.

Although tender engines started to receive large transferred numbers in place of the 6½″ brass figures in 1905, the changeover on tank engines did not start until 1909. No. 1844 has had its 1907 number applied without any attention in the paint shop and the outline of the old figures (2012) can clearly be seen underneath. Built in 1892 by Vulcan Foundry, the locomotive was a late survivor, being withdrawn in April 1964 as BR 41844. When photographed at Leeds shed, it carried crimson lake livery with simplified lining: only the front boiler band is possibly lined. The tank lining is carried round to the front panels.

In 1871, Beyer, Peacock built a class of ten 4′ 2″ shunters with 16″ x 24″ cylinders, numbered 800-809. All were put on the duplicate A list in 1890 and re-built with Johnson cabs and class A boilers in 1895-7, the condition in which No. 881A is seen here. Re-numbered 1610-19 in 1907, all survived the grouping but were withdrawn by 1927, 881A being the last survivor. Lining above the running plate appears to be restricted to the boiler bands, with two yellow lines on the tanks; one immediately inside the rivets and a second one 4″ inboard. The axle ends, wheel centres and sand boxes also carry the simple lining.

At first sight there is nothing unusual about this Johnson 0-6-0T, one of 280 similar locomotives built between 1874 and 1900. However No. 1346 only existed as such for three years, having been built as No. 223 in 1890. In 1904 its number was given to a Vulcan Foundry built Kirtley 0-6-0, the original number of which (843) was required for a new Belpaire 4-4-0. The logic of this was that an earlier batch of tanks included a number series 1347 et seq. and this can be seen as an attempt to tidy up the largely random numbering system. In 1907 the matter was taken in hand with Deeley's total re-numbering scheme, and 1346 became 1766. Some non-vacuum braked goods engines were for a short period painted brown and lined out black; a colour sample of the brown is given in Midland Style. Some Kirtley double-framed goods engines were painted unlined crimson lake.